KU-601-247

Peoples of the Arctic

Robert Low

FRANKLIN WATTS
NEW YORK • LONDON • SYDNEY

This edition first published in the UK in 1997 by
Franklin Watts
96 Leonard Street
London
EC2A 4RH

© 1996 The Rosen Publishing Group, Inc., New York

Picture credits: Cover © P. Halley/ANAKO Editions; pp. 4,
16 © M. Poirel & C. Raoult/ANAKO Editions; p. 7 © Van Der hilst/Gamma Liaison;
pp. 8, 11 © P. Halley/ANAKO Edition; p. 12 © Wolfgang Kaehler/Gamma Liaison;
p. 15 © Stein P. Aasheim/Gamma Liaison; pp. 19, 20 © Erik Sampers/Gamma Liaison.

A CIP catalogue record for this book is available from the British Library.

ISBN 0 7496 2865 0

Printed in the United States of America

Contents

What is the Arctic? 5

Peoples of the Arctic 6

Plants and animals 9

Living in the Arctic 10

Food and clothes 13

Hunting, fishing and farming 14

Getting about 17

Building a home 18

Families and communities 21

Changing times 22

Glossary 23

Index 24

What is the Arctic?

The Arctic is the far north, at the top of the earth. Some parts are so cold that the ground is covered with snow all year round, and water is always frozen. Other parts **thaw,** but only in the summer.

In the winter the sun does not rise, so it is dark all day and night. But in the summer the opposite happens. The sun does not set for long, so it is daylight almost all the time.

◀ Much of the Arctic is frozen all year round.

Peoples of the Arctic

Although it is so cold, people do live in the Arctic. The Inuit, once called Eskimos, live in the Arctic area of North America. The Sami, once called Lapps, live in the Arctic area of Europe. The Yakut and the Chukchi live in the Arctic area of Asia.

These people live on different **continents** and speak different languages. But they all know how to **survive** in the cold Arctic weather.

The Sami live in Lapland, the ▶ Arctic region of Europe.

Plants and animals

Many animals that live in the Arctic, such as reindeer, polar bears and huskies (a kind of dog), have thick fur to keep them warm.

Whales, seals and walruses live in the freezing Arctic Ocean. Their bodies have a thick layer of fat to keep them warm.

The Arctic is too cold for most plants. But a few mosses, grasses and tiny shrubs grow where it thaws in summer.

◀ Some Arctic peoples, such as the Inuit, use huskies to pull sledges.

Living in the Arctic

Life is difficult for the people who live in the Arctic. The land is frozen and very cold for most of the year and travelling is almost impossible in the winter.

To survive, Arctic peoples have learned to get what they need from the **environment** in which they live.

Arctic peoples wear animal furs to keep themselves ▶
warm in the long, cold Arctic winter.

Food and clothes

Long ago, meat and fish were the only food Arctic peoples had. And they had to catch it themselves. Today, shops in Arctic towns stock food from all over the world.

Arctic peoples used to make their clothes from the skins of the animals they hunted for food. Today they can buy warm clothes made of other materials. But some still prefer the traditional sealskin boots, bearskin trousers and reindeer-skin jackets.

◀ Warm fur hoods help keep faces and ears warm in the Arctic winter.

Hunting, fishing and farming

In the past most Arctic peoples got their food by hunting and fishing. The Inuit used **harpoons** to catch seals. Today, they also use rifles to hunt land animals such as reindeer and bears. But fishermen still have to cut holes in the ice before they can start fishing!

The Sami are farmers. They keep reindeer which eat the moss and grass that grow where the snow melts in summer.

Like the Sami, some Chukchi ▶ still keep reindeer.

Getting about

The traditional way to travel over the snow-covered ground was by sledge. Each sledge was pulled by a team of huskies. Snowmobiles are more popular now.

To travel by water, the Inuit used boats called **kayaks** and **umiaks**. Kayaks hold one person, umiaks can take several people. Paddles are used to drive the boats through the water. Today, the Inuit also use motorboats.

◀ Today, many people in the Arctic travel around on snowmobiles.

Building a home

Arctic peoples built homes from whatever materials were available. In the far north, the Inuit made round houses called **igloos** out of snow and ice blocks. The Sami lived in tents made of reindeer skin.

Today, most people living in the Arctic build their homes from wood imported from other countries. Now the Inuit only make igloos when they are on long hunting trips.

Tents made of reindeer skin are light ▶
to carry and quick to put up.

Families and communities

Life in the Arctic is so tough that people have to rely on each other for support and help. Families stick together.

Inuit grandparents often live with their children and grandchildren. Grandmothers help care for their young grandchildren.

Sami families often travel and work together when they take care of their herds of reindeer.

◀ The Yakut show their pride in their community by wearing traditional dress for a national celebration.

Changing times

Today, many Arctic people live in wooden houses with electric light and television. Telephone lines link villages to towns and cities. Aeroplanes take mail and supplies to distant villages, and sometimes help to find reindeer herds. People buy food and clothes in shops and department stores. Children go to schools like yours.

Life has changed in the Arctic, but the weather is just as cold!

Glossary

continents The largest areas of land on earth: Europe, Africa, Asia, Australasia, Antarctica, North and South America.

environment Your surroundings.

harpoon Weapon like a spear, which has a sharp tip, a long pole and a rope attached to it.

igloo Round house made of ice and snow.

kayak Light one-person canoe made of sealskins over a wooden frame.

survive To find a way to live.

thaw To warm up, so that ice and snow melt.

umiak Boat made by the Inuit. It is larger than a kayak.

Index

A
Arctic Ocean, 9

C
Chukchi, 6, 13, 14
clothes, 13
continent, 6, 23

E
environment, 10, 23

F
families, 21
farming, 14
fishing, 14
food, 13, 14

H
harpoons, 14, 23
hunting, 14
huskies, 9, 17

I
igloos, 18, 23
Inuit, 6, 14, 17, 18, 21

K
kayak, 17, 23

P
plants, 9, 14
polar bears, 9

R
reindeer, 9, 14, 18, 21, 22

S
Sami, 6, 14, 18, 21
seals, 9, 14
snow, 5, 14
summer, 5, 14
sun, 5

T
thaw, 5, 23

U
umiak, 17, 23

W
winter, 5

Y
Yakut, 6, 21